Extracting the Precious From
Isaiah

Bethany House Books
by Donna Partow

Becoming a Vessel God Can Use
Becoming a Vessel God Can Use Prayer Journal
Becoming the Woman I Want to Be
Living in Absolute Freedom
Standing Firm
This Isn't the Life I Signed Up For
This Isn't the Life I Signed Up For AudioBook
This Isn't the Life I Signed Up For Growth Guide
Walking in Total God-Confidence
A Woman's Guide to Personality Types

EXTRACTING THE PRECIOUS
2 Corinthians
Isaiah
Galatians
Nehemiah

EXTRACTING THE PRECIOUS
A BIBLE STUDY FOR WOMEN

Extracting the Precious From
Isaiah

Donna Partow
with Lin Johnson

BETHANYHOUSE
Minneapolis, Minnesota

Published by Bethany House Publishers
11400 Hampshire Avenue South
Bloomington, Minnesota 55438

Bethany House Publishers is a division of
Baker Publishing Group, Grand Rapids, Michigan.

Printed in the United States of America

ISBN-13:   978-0-7642-2697-7
ISBN-10:   0-7642-2697-5

Library of Congress Cataloging-in-Publication Data

Partow, Donna.
    Extracting the precious from Isaiah : a Bible study for women / by Donna Partow with Lin Johnson.
        p.   cm.
    ISBN 0-7642-2697-5 (pbk.)
    1. Bible. O.T. Isaiah—Criticism, interpretation, etc.   2. Bible. O.T. Isaiah—Study and teaching.   I. Johnson, Lin.   II. Title.
    BS1515.52.P37   2003
    224'.1'0071 dc21

                                                                          2003013786

DONNA PARTOW is a Christian communicator with a compelling testimony of God's transforming power. Her uncommon transparency and passion for Christ have been used by God at women's conferences and retreats throughout North America. She is the bestselling author of numerous books and has been a popular guest on more than two hundred radio and TV programs, including *Focus on the Family*.

If your church sponsors an annual women's conference or retreat, perhaps they would be interested in learning more about the author's special weekend programs. For more information, contact:

Donna Partow
Web site: *www.donnapartow.com*

LIN JOHNSON is managing editor of *The Christian Communicator, Advanced Christian Writer,* and *Church Libraries.* She has written over sixty books, specializing in Bible curriculum, and is a Gold Medallion Book Award recipient. Lin directs the Write-to-Publish Conference in the Chicago area and teaches at conferences across the country and internationally. She resides near Chicago. Her Web site is *www.wordprocommunications.com.*

Contents

Preface

EXTRACTING THE PRECIOUS
Bible Study Series

This Bible study series began the day it finally dawned on me that there were two ways to learn the life lessons God has in store for us: the easy way and the hard way. Personally, I've always specialized in learning my lessons the hard way, through painful life experiences. Sure, I've learned a lot, but I've got the battle scars to prove it too. The easy way to learn is sitting at the feet of Jesus, meditating upon His Word. The longer I walk with God, the more determined I become to learn directly from Him—sitting quietly in the privacy of my prayer room rather than learning as I get jostled around out there in the cold, cruel world. Which way would you rather learn?

I used to think I was "getting away with something" when I neglected the spiritual disciplines such as prayer, Bible study, Scripture memorization, and participating in a small group study. But I was only deceiving myself. The plain and simple fact is this: We all reap what we sow. Nothing more, nothing less. God won't force you to study your Bible. He won't come down from heaven and clobber you over the head if you skip some of the questions in this book. He won't even be mad at you if you put this down right now and never pick it up again. In fact, God will love you the exact same amount. His unfailing love for you is completely unconditional.

But God's love doesn't wipe out the logical consequences of our choices. Here's how Deuteronomy 30:19–20 puts it:

*This day I call heaven and earth as witnesses against
you that I have set before you life and death, blessings and
curses. Now choose life, so that you and your children may
live and that you may love the Lord your God, listen to
His voice, and hold fast to him.*

Reading God's Word is the ultimate choice for life, not only for
us but to those who will come after us. Every moment we choose
to spend searching, meditating, memorizing is a choice for life.
Every moment we neglect His Word, we are choosing death—the
death of our spiritual and personal potential; the death of an oppor-
tunity to become all God desires us to be. God's love is unconditional, but His blessings are not. Here's how the psalmist put it:

*Blessed is the man
who does not walk in the counsel of the wicked
or stand in the way of sinners
or sit in the seat of mockers.
But his delight is in the law of the Lord,
and on his law he meditates day and night.
He is like a tree planted by streams of water,
which yields its fruit in season
and whose leaf does not wither.
Whatever he does prospers.*
—Psalm 1:1–3

God says we will be blessed (happy, fortunate, prosperous, and
enviable) if we spend more time in His Word and less time with
clueless people (my paraphrase). Does that mean we'll never have
to learn anything the hard way? Not quite! Let's face it: certain class-
es require a "hands-on" component. I couldn't graduate from chem-
istry class without stepping into the lab, putting on my scientist-
wanna-be (or in my case, scientist-never-gonna-be) coat, and
conducting some of those experiments for myself. At the same time,
I found that my ability to conduct those experiments successfully
was directly linked to the amount of time I spent studying the text-
book in advance. You can't learn what it is to be a parent without

having children underfoot. Neither can you fully comprehend God's faithfulness without finding yourself trapped in the middle of a real-world situation where nothing else can see you through. Nevertheless, there is much we *can* learn in solitude and study of God's Word so when we encounter various tests in life, we'll be well-prepared to experience a successful outcome. Jeremiah 15:19 is a passage that has always been especially meaningful to me:

> *Therefore, thus says the Lord,*
> *"If you return, then I will restore you—*
> *Before Me you will stand;*
> *And if you extract the precious from the worthless,*
> *You will become My spokesman."*
> *—Jeremiah 15:19* NASB

The first time I heard those words, my heart leapt within me and I said, "Yes, Lord, I want to extract the precious from every worthless circumstance I must endure!" I was instantly overtaken with a holy determination to learn all I could from every class I landed in at the School of Hard Knocks.

Those of you who are familiar with my work know I've built my writing and speaking ministry on story illustrations and life lessons gleaned from my various follies and foibles. My friends all tease me whenever they see me embroiled in yet another mess, "Don't worry, Donna. You'll get through this . . . and turn it into a great illustration." And they're right! I always do. But with this new series, I wanted to do something entirely different. I wanted my readers to know that just as we can extract the precious from the worthless, we can extract the precious from the precious too! Rather than telling you my stories, I wanted you to read His story. You can learn to glean story illustrations and life lessons while sitting peacefully at His feet rather than getting bloodied out in the street. Isn't that a beautiful thought?

The other thing I wanted to share with you is this: I love learning from other people, but I'd much rather learn from God. As much as I enjoy reading Christian books, completing various Bible studies, listening to teaching tapes, and attending conferences, nothing on earth compares to those moments when I realize God has cut out the middle man. When it's just Him, His Word, and me. He is serving as my personal tutor. That's when His Word truly comes alive for me. And that's what I want you to experience for yourself with the EXTRACTING THE PRECIOUS studies. I want to get out of the way as much as possible and let God teach you directly from His Word. You'll notice that I've saved my pithy little comments for the end of each chapter, so you aren't biased by my perspective on what's important. You can decide that for yourself.

USING THIS STUDY GUIDE

Every book in this series will feature twelve chapters, each of which is divided into three sections:

Search the Word features a series of inductive Bible study questions designed to help you interact with the Bible text. Use a Bible version that is easy to understand. I recommend the New International Version, but if you prefer a different version (e.g., New King James, New American Standard, *New Living Translation*), that's fine. You may enjoy reading from several translations, and if you're a true scholar, the *Amplified Bible* is ideal for studying a passage in depth. You may want to complete each study in two or three sittings rather than answering all the questions at once. Then, instead of simply copying the Bible text, answer the questions in your own words.

Consider the Message provides a narrative section that illustrates the truth of the chapter, showing how it can be lived out in today's world.

Apply the Truth contains questions to help you apply the biblical teaching to your daily life, along with a verse or short passage to memorize. Depend on the Holy Spirit to guide and help you with these questions so He can pinpoint areas of your life where God wants you to practice His truth.

Although I suspect many of you will be using these books for your personal quiet time, I have included a brief Leader's Guide at the end of each book. It includes some background information on the Bible text, along with cross-references and suggestions for using this study guide in a group setting.

I want you to know how excited I am for you as you begin this journey with God and His Word. You will soon discover (if you don't know this already) that the truths you glean on your own will ultimately have far greater impact on your life than anything you've ever learned secondhand. People died to give us the right to study God's Word for ourselves. It's a great privilege. Make the most of it. As you do, here's my prayer for you:

For this reason I kneel before the Father, from whom his whole family in heaven and on earth derives its name. I pray that out of his glorious riches he may strengthen you with power through his Spirit in your inner being, so that Christ may dwell in your hearts through faith. And I pray that you, being rooted and established in love, may have power, together with all the saints, to grasp how wide and long and high and deep is the love of Christ, and to know this love that surpasses knowledge—that you may be filled to the measure of all the fullness of God.

Now to him who is able to do immeasurably more than all we ask or imagine, according to his power that is at work within us, to him be glory in the church and in Christ Jesus throughout all generations, for ever and ever! Amen.

—Ephesians 3:14–21

Blessings,
His Vessel
Donna Partow

Introduction

A Glimpse of God's Faithfulness

I was stranded at the Sacramento airport several years ago. My first inclination was to pitch a mental fit, in my usual fashion: bemoaning my fate, wondering why on earth this stuff *always* happens to me. . . . But I thought better of it and decided to make the most of an otherwise frustrating situation. I managed to find a relatively quiet spot, sat down, and opened my Bible to the first chapter of Isaiah. I don't know how to describe what happened next, other than to say the words came to life before me. It was absolutely electrifying. The buzz of the airport faded into the distance as passage after passage pulsed through my spirit. God's Word became truly living and active in me.

Perhaps the most fascinating part was the way in which God's Spirit illuminated all my hand-written margin notes—those things I had jotted down during various sermons over the years. Obviously, I had thought the information was significant enough at the time to write it down. But something very different was happening. What was once merely interesting, having been given to me secondhand, suddenly took on profound meaning as God showed me, firsthand, exactly what it meant *for me*.

That day at the Sacramento airport, I grabbed hold of something I had always known but never really thought about: the profound difference between secondhand information and firsthand illumination when it comes to the study of God's Word. Ever since that day, Isaiah has been one of my favorite books of the Bible. That's why I chose to include it in the EXTRACTING THE PRECIOUS series. (By the way, I was able to read all sixty-six chapters in one sitting. It can be done fairly easily, and I highly recommend you do so before proceeding with this chapter-by-chapter study.) I pray that the book of Isaiah will come to life for you in an electrifying, life-changing way. Before you dive in, however, let's examine some background information, which will help you as you begin your own study of Isaiah.

The Man

When we think of prophets, we usually think of someone like John the Baptist—a wild-looking man, wandering around in the desert wearing a camel-hair shirt, munching grasshoppers. If that's what you picture when you imagine Isaiah, you couldn't be more wrong. According to Chuck Swindoll, Isaiah's "eloquent literary style, distinguished Jewish upbringing, and tireless declaration of God's Word have earned him the titles 'Prince Among Prophets' and 'Saint Paul of the Old Testament.'"[1] Isaiah, from all appearances, was born into an aristocratic Jewish family that provided him with an outstanding education. He spent most of his life in the city of Jerusalem, routinely meeting with kings and other prominent political and religious officials. He was held in great esteem by the vast majority of people. Isaiah was married to a prophetess and had at least two sons. His ministry lasted nearly sixty years—an incredible feat when one considers the substance of his message and the propensity of all political leaders to "shoot the messenger." It would seem that, ultimately, Isaiah was put to death because of his stand for righteousness. Tradition says that Isaiah was sawed in half, at the age of 120, during the reign of King Manasseh (see Hebrews 11:37).

Historical Context

For five hundred years, from the tenth to the fifth century B.C., God sent prophets to warn His people of impending judgment. The following passage from 2 Kings 17 vividly sets the stage for the book of Isaiah, explaining exactly why God was about to turn His people over to their enemies. Please read it carefully, as it will help you tremendously as you undertake the study of Isaiah.

All this took place because the Israelites had sinned
against the Lord their God, who had brought them up out
of Egypt from under the power of Pharaoh king of Egypt.
They worshiped other gods and followed the practices of
the nations the Lord had driven out before them, as well as
the practices that the kings of Israel had introduced. The
Israelites secretly did things against the Lord their God
that were not right. From watchtower to fortified city they
built themselves high places in all their towns. They set up
sacred stones and Asherah poles on every high hill and
under every spreading tree. At every high place they
burned incense, as the nations whom the Lord had driven
out before them had done. They did wicked things that pro-
voked the Lord to anger. They worshiped idols, though the
Lord had said, "You shall not do this." The Lord warned
Israel and Judah through all his prophets and seers: "Turn
from your evil ways. Observe my commands and decrees,
in accordance with the entire Law that I commanded your
fathers to obey and that I delivered to you through my ser-
vants the prophets."

But they would not listen and were as stiff-necked as
their fathers, who did not trust in the Lord their God. They
rejected his decrees and the covenant he had made with
their fathers and the warnings he had given them. They
followed worthless idols and themselves became worthless.
They imitated the nations around them although the Lord
had ordered them, "Do not do as they do," and they did
the things the Lord had forbidden them to do.

They forsook all the commands of the Lord their God
and made for themselves two idols cast in the shape of
calves, and an Asherah pole. They bowed down to all the
starry hosts, and they worshiped Baal. They sacrificed
their sons and daughters in the fire. They practiced divina-
tion and sorcery and sold themselves to do evil in the eyes

of the Lord, provoking him to anger.
So the Lord was very angry with Israel and removed
them from his presence. Only the tribe of Judah was left,
and even Judah did not keep the commands of the Lord
their God. They followed the practices Israel had intro-
duced. Therefore the Lord rejected all the people of Israel;
he afflicted them and gave them into the hands of plunder-
ers, until he thrust them from his presence.
—2 Kings 17:7–20

Whoa! Harsh words indeed. But when we consider all the
mighty miracles God had performed on behalf of His people, and
His faithfulness in delivering them from Egypt, leading them
through the desert, then bringing them into their Promised Land,
we realize that God is right in His judgment. The worship of idols
involved such sexual depravity and heartless violence we can hardly
even imagine it in our day. We think sexual depravity means an
engaged couple having intercourse before their wedding day. God's
people engaged in giant orgies, conducted in public places in full
view of their children—and had the gall to call it a "worship service." We are appalled by abortion. These people made their tod-
dlers walk into a blazing furnace, watched them burn alive. Be sure
to keep all of that in mind when you hear the words of judgment
Isaiah is about to utter against these people. They weren't just falling
short of the mark. It's not that they weren't devoting enough time to
Bible study or forgot to vote in the last election. They engaged in
evil that is truly mind-boggling. The next time people at your
church complain about how the world is going downhill, tell them
to reread the Old Testament. Enough said!

The Time in Which He Lived

By the time Isaiah burst on the scene as God's prophet in 740
B.C., the nation of Israel had long been divided into the Northern
and Southern Kingdoms. After Solomon's death a bloody civil war
had split the nation in two (in 931 B.C.), with Israel in the North
and Judah in the South. Isaiah prophesied to the Southern Kingdom

during the reigns of four kings: Uzziah, Jotham, Ahaz, and Hezekiah. You can read 2 Kings 14–21 in its entirety for more historical background. The prophets Hosea and Micah were his contemporaries, with Hosea prophesying to the Northern Kingdom and Micah to the Southern Kingdom. Isaiah's ministry spanned the last seventeen years of the Northern Kingdom of Israel before the Assyrians took the people into captivity in 722 B.C. The people of Judah were following the same path of sin away from God and would be taken into captivity later by the Babylonians in 586 B.C.

In addition to the sexual depravity described above, their society was marked by political corruption and social indifference. The rich were filthy rich, and the poor were filthy with poverty. And no one cared . . . but God. He saw the suffering inflicted upon the *have-nots* by the *haves,* and it broke His heart. The people of Judah trampled the poor underfoot and then went to God's temple to sacrifice a sheep, donate a burnt offering, and congratulate themselves on their adherence to the letter of the law. God was no more impressed by their hypocrisy than He is with our hypocrisy today.

The Book

Isaiah spoke courageously to the people of his own day. Yet, as a visionary prophet, he also spoke of a day still to come, culminating in his breathtaking description of the coming Messiah and, beyond that, the future kingdom when the suffering Savior will return to rule in splendor and glory. In addition, the book of Isaiah presents a fascinating microcosm of the Bible. Consider this: The entire Bible consists of sixty-six books. The first thirty-nine comprise the Old Testament, which presents the law as God's holy requirement and God's judgment on His people for their inability to fulfill the law. The next twenty-seven books, the New Testament, present a new covenant, through which God offers salvation for sin, as Jesus fulfills the law's requirement and offers himself as the spotless Lamb of God, sacrificed for the redemption of our sins.

In the same way, the book of Isaiah divides neatly into two sections. Chapters 1–39 deal with judgment for sin, while chapters 40–66 deal with the comfort of salvation. Here's how Henrietta Mears describes it in her must-read book *What the Bible Is All About.*

> *The Old Testament opens with God's case against humans because of their sin. Isaiah opens the same way (Isaiah 1:18). The first section closes with the prophecy of the coming King of Righteousness and the redemption of Israel, just as the prophets close the Old Testament with the prediction of His coming kingdom. The second part of Isaiah opens with the "voice of him that crieth in the wilderness" (John the Baptist), and is concerned with the person and work of Jesus Christ. The New Testament opens in exact accord with this. John the Baptist, the forerunner of Jesus, is announced (John 1:6, 23). Isaiah ends with the vision of new heavens and a new earth wherein dwelleth righteousness. The New Testament closes with this same view in Revelation. This striking similarity between Isaiah and the whole Bible is unforgettable when once mastered.*[2]

Throughout the book, God's faithfulness shines brightly. Although Isaiah spoke primarily to the nation of Judah, his messages included judgment of other nations and God's offer of salvation to all who would turn to Him. Like other Old Testament prophetic books, Isaiah's messages focused on a variety of time periods: the present (threatening captivities by Assyria and Babylon), future (restoration of the nation after captivity), and distant future (the first and second comings of the Messiah). The context and content help us determine to which period a message is most relevant.

Although this study guide deals with only twelve chapters of Isaiah, you will benefit tremendously by reading the entire book as you complete this study. Reading Isaiah's words in their entirety will give you a fuller picture of God's faithfulness and, more important, greater confidence in the God who is faithful. I pray it will bless your heart both now and for years to come.

Session One
Isaiah 1

God's Faithfulness Delivers Us From Hypocrisy

SEARCH THE WORD

1 Describe a time when you knew you were acting like a hypocrite (or perhaps someone accused you of being one). What motives were driving your actions and attitudes?

> **To profess to love God while leading an unholy life is the worst of falsehoods.**
> —augustine

It's easy to become a religious hypocrite, putting on a good show for other people even though God sees our hearts and knows better. In fact, God's people in Isaiah's day were poster children for the need to match inward reality with outward actions in the religious realm. So God addressed that need at the beginning of this book. Read and meditate on Isaiah 1.

Read verses 1-9.

2 With what tone did God begin His message to the people of Judah? Why?

3 What comparisons did He use to highlight the people's sinfulness?

4 In light of this opening description of the people to whom God sent Isaiah, how would you word a classified ad for his job?

5 What do you learn about God and His faithfulness from this passage?

Read verses 10-15.

6 Everything God mentioned here was required in the Law. So why did God condemn the people's religious rituals?

7 If God were writing this message to us today, what would He say?

Read verses 16-20.

8 What was God's response to the people's religious hypocrisy?

9 In contrast, what kind of life did God want them to live?

10 How can we obey these commands today?

11 What options did God offer, and what were the conditions attached to them?

> The greatest single cause of atheism in the world today is Christians who acknowledge Jesus with their lips and then walk out the door and deny Him by their lifestyle. That is what an unbelieving world simply finds unbelievable.
>
> –dc taLk

12 Why is it harder to live the kind of life God prescribed here than to go through the motions of religious activity?

Read verses 21-23.

13 In what ways had the city of Jerusalem changed from the days of kings David and Solomon?

14 Why was God so upset about these changes?

Read verses 24-31.

15 How will God's judgment on Jerusalem affect Him?

16 What part will God play in restoring the city and people to himself?

17 What do these pictures convey about the people's future?

CONSIDER THE MESSAGE

One of the most chilling moments of my life occurred when I arrived at a dear friend's house, only to discover that moments before she had taken a deliberate overdose of drugs in a desperate suicide attempt. She lived in the middle of nowhere, with no hospital in sight. We jumped into my car, and as we sped through the darkness, her life hung in the balance. I honestly didn't know if she would live or die. I had invited her to church many times to no avail, although she had attended a Christian concert with me earlier that same year. I had told her over and over again that "Jesus was the answer" to her problems. Now as she looked at me through a drug-induced fog, she muttered, "If I make it through this, I promise I'm gonna get it together. I'm gonna get my act together and start going to church with you."

I was stunned. *How could she be so deceived that she thought she had to clean herself up before she could come to God?* I thought. *Where on earth had she gotten a stupid idea like that?* Then a still, small voice within me replied, *"From you, Donna. From you."* In my zeal to demonstrate that "Jesus was the answer," I had gone too far . . . pretending I had all the answers too. I thought being a good witness meant never letting on that I still had plenty of problems of my own. In short, I had become a hypocrite.

The world is fed up with Christians trying to sell them quick, easy solutions to complex problems. They need to see something REAL in our lives! If we're going to break free from the snare of hypocrisy, we will have to admit we don't have all the answers. We haven't arrived. We don't have the perfect marriage or the perfect children or the perfect church. We're sinners just like everyone else. Our lives will have far greater impact when we're willing to admit to the world around us, "Hey, I blow it every day of my life, but I'm not who I used to be, and I'm not who I would have been."

God doesn't like hypocrites either. If you have any doubts about that, this chapter from Isaiah should lay them to rest. You might also check out Jesus' remarks in Matthew 6:1–18 and 15:1–20. God doesn't want us to act like a bunch of know-it-alls, yet that's precisely how many Christians behave. In fact, the only thing we need to know for sure is that Jesus Christ has done something incredible for us and that, as a result of His sacrifice, God has washed our sins "white as snow" (Isaiah 1:18).

As we ponder God's faithfulness in the coming weeks, it is my prayer that God will deliver you from all remnants of hypocrisy. That you'll no longer feel the need to pretend to be someone you're not. As you grow in understanding of how great God is and all He has done, you will be increasingly aware that there is nothing you can add to God. He doesn't need you to enhance His reputation with outward displays of religiosity. God doesn't need you to turn in a shining performance for Him. Indeed, I believe God's faithfulness shines forth most brightly not through our perfection but through our imperfections. Then people will realize, "Hey,

Christians really aren't perfect, just forgiven. If God has accepted them just as they are, I can believe He'll accept me just as I am." It's not just a bumper sticker, friends, it's the truth. Let's live like we believe it.

APPLY THE TRUTH

1 How is having faith in God different from belonging to a church or Bible study group?

2 Spend time in prayer, asking God to show you the truth about your spiritual life. Is your Christianity just a package of religious activities? To answer that question, you might contrast how much time is spent in public practice versus private practice. How much of your Christian walk is driven by the opinion of others (i.e., what people think a good Christian 'ought' to do) and how much is driven internally by a heart that's seeking after God in your private prayer closet?

> Have mercy on me, O God, according to your unfailing love; according to your great compassion blot out my transgressions. Wash away all my iniquity and cleanse me from my sin. For I know my transgressions, and my sin is always before me. Against you, you only, have I sinned and done what is evil in your sight, so that you are proved right when you speak and justified when you judge.
> –psaLm 51:1-4

3 A growing awareness of God's faithfulness can deliver you from hypocrisy, but it's up to you to change your focus from outward performance to inward reality. That will mean caring less about what other people *think* is true about your life and caring far more about what God *knows* is true about your heart. What changes do you

need to make to bring your heart and actions in line with what pleases God?

4 Choose which change you will work on this week. Write a strategy describing how, when, and where you can begin to do so.

5 Memorize Isaiah 1:17–18:

Learn to do right!
Seek justice,
encourage the oppressed.
Defend the cause of the fatherless,
plead the case of the widow.
"Come now, let us reason together,"
says the Lord.
"Though your sins are like scarlet,
they shall be as white as snow;
though they are red as crimson,
they shall be like wool."

You will find the memory verses printed at the back of this book. I encourage you to cut them out and tuck them in your purse. Whenever you have a free moment, pull them out and review them.

Session Two
Isaiah 6

God's Faithfulness Calls Us to Spiritual Cleansing and to Service

SEARCH THE WORD

1 Here's a test you can take to see whether or not you are allowing the Holy Spirit to do His work of cleansing in your life: What specific sin did the Holy Spirit convict you of this past week? What specific thing did you do or say—or fail to do or say—that the Holy Spirit revealed needed acknowledgment and repentance?

How did you respond? Why?

I'd like to suggest to you that if you don't have an answer to the above question, it ain't 'cause you didn't sin! It's because you are not cooperating with the purposes of God in bringing about spiritual cleansing in your life. Every one of us sins every day. The closer we draw to God, the more we realize the dramatic contrast between His perfect holiness and our sinfulness. When Isaiah saw God in 740 B.C., the year King Uzziah died, he also saw his need for cleansing and gave us a powerful example to follow. Read and meditate on Isaiah 6.

Read verses 1–4.

2 What did Isaiah see and hear before God called him to proclaim His message?

3 What did he learn about God from this vision?

> Our sense of sin is in proportion to our nearness to God.
> –thomas d. bernard

Read verses 5–7.

4 How did this vision affect Isaiah? Why?

5 What is significant about the way Isaiah described God?

6 How did God cleanse Isaiah's sin?

7 Why was this cleansing necessary?

Read verses 8-10.

8 After God cleansed Isaiah, what did He call Isaiah to do?

9 How did Isaiah respond?

> **Unlike Adam and Eve, who sought to hide from the searching voice, Isaiah, permitted for a moment to eavesdrop on the councils of God, cannot keep silent. "Would I do?" Such a grateful offering of themselves is always the cry of those who have received God's grace after they have given up hope of ever being acceptable to God.**
>
> –john n. oswaLt[1]

10 How was Isaiah's response different from how he first reacted to the vision? What made the difference?

11 What assignment did God give Isaiah?

12 How would the people respond to his message? Why?

13 If you had been Isaiah, what would you have said to God? Why?

Before Isaiah could go, he had to grieve—over his sin, over the sins of his nation, over the infinite gulf that lay between himself and a holy God. Before he could be sent, he had to be cleansed. Christ has commissioned us to take the gospel message to the world (Matthew 28:18-20). But spreading the true gospel requires knowing the true God—all of his attributes, from his consuming holiness to His cleansing grace. We must balance the going with the knowing. In fact, we're not really ready to go until we know.
—charLes swindoLl

Read verses 11-13.

14 After God's response to Isaiah in verses 9–10, what did Isaiah ask Him? Why?

15 How did God's answer both discourage Isaiah and give him hope?

CONSIDER THE MESSAGE

If we were ever to encounter God as Isaiah did in this chapter, we would have the same reaction: "'Woe to me!' I cried. 'I am ruined! For I am a man of unclean lips, and I live among a people of unclean lips, and my eyes have seen the King, the LORD Almighty'" (v. 5). Very few of us will experience such a powerful moment, but I believe all of us eventually come to the same realization. The more we know of God, the more we recognize our own sinfulness. That's why people we would consider giants in the faith spend *more* time in confession and repentance than new believers do. What they once considered "no big deal" or covered under the protection of "everybody does it" is now viewed as an affront to a holy God. Our sin must be dealt with in three steps.

First, we confront it.

Next, we confess it.

Then, God cleanses it (1 John 1:9).

So when you are confronted with the truth about sin in your life, be thankful: you are on the path to spiritual cleansing. As we cooperate with God, we experience ever-increasing degrees of personal holiness. In the early stages of our Christian lives, we recognize the need to be cleansed of our sinful acts. Next, the Holy Spirit shines the light of truth on our sinful attitudes or those things we ought to have done but neglected to do. Ultimately, we realize we must be cleansed, not only of our own sins but of our sinful response to the sin of others.

Sadly, many Christians congratulate themselves if they aren't committing blatant *sins of behavior* like those "worldly" people. They don't drink, abuse drugs, gamble, or engage in illicit sex. Unfortunately, they overlook the greater significance God places on *sins of the heart.* They think nothing of their indifference—their ability to cross the street so they can avoid seeing human suffering, just like the cold-hearted religious leaders Jesus condemned in the parable of the Good Samaritan. Nor are they bothered by the fact that their hearts are hardened by a critical, judgmental attitude that knows what's wrong with everyone in the world—except the person in the mirror. They are like the Pharisees of Jesus' day who were very careful about following a prescribed set of rules and behavior patterns— and looked down their spiritual noses at anyone else who didn't follow the rules. They are like the older brother in the parable of the Prodigal Son—they are in the father's house, but far from the father's heart of compassion for the lost.

I believe the Holy Spirit is calling God's people, even now, to cooperate with Him in the process of spiritual cleansing. If, in the past, you've only repented of your actions, He wants you to repent of your inaction as well. If you've only dealt with sins of behavior, He wants you to confront the truth about the sins of your heart. He wants to take you deeper still. He wants to show you that very often our sinful response to the sin of others can be more damaging, more defiling than the sin that was originally committed. Sins like gossip, anger, resentment, and a holier-than-thou attitude often do more damage to the average Christian home than drugs or R-rated movies could ever do.

> **Repentance means altering one's habits of thought, one's attitudes, outlook, policy, direction, and behavior, just as fully as is needed to get one's life out of the wrong shape and into the right one.**
> **Repentance is in truth a spiritual revolution.**
> —j. i. packer[3]

Today when you come before God in prayer, don't bring a list with you. So often we are only concerned with our needs and wants and demands. Instead, let's focus entirely on Him. Let's enter His presence and keep quiet, allowing Him to reveal himself to us in a new and personal way. In addition to today's passage, you might want to meditate on Psalm 51, a psalm of repentance and brokenness, written by David after he had been confronted about the truth of his sin. May the words he penned be used by God to confront each of us with the truth about our sin as well.

APPLY THE TRUTH

1 What did you learn about God from this chapter?

About sin?

About God's call?

2 Spend some time in prayer, asking God to show you himself and your sin. Then ask Him to cleanse you from that sin.

3 Now ask God what He's calling you to do. Listen for His answer. Can you respond like Isaiah did? If not, why not?

4 Memorize Isaiah 6:5–8:

> "Woe to me!" I cried. "I am ruined! For I am a man of unclean lips, and I live among a people of unclean lips, and my eyes have seen the King, the LORD Almighty."
> Then one of the seraphs flew to me with a live coal in his hand, which he had taken with tongs from the altar. With it he touched my mouth and said, "See, this has touched your lips; your guilt is taken away and your sin atoned for."
> Then I heard the voice of the Lord saying, "Whom shall I send? And who will go for us?"
> And I said, "Here am I. Send me!"

Session Three
Isaiah 26

God's Faithfulness
Elicits Praise

SEARCH THE WORD

1 For what do you praise God the most? Why?

The measure of our praise is an accurate barometer of our knowledge of God. The more we know of who He is and what He can do, the more our hearts will overflow with spontaneous praise. The book of Isaiah is filled with praise of God, such as the song presented in Isaiah 26. Read the entire chapter now and meditate on it.

> **Had I a thousand tongues, I would praise God with them all.**
> —peter boehLer

Read verses 1-6.

2 How did Isaiah describe the city of the New Jerusalem?

3 Who will live in this city?

4 What is the secret to experiencing peace in times of trouble?

5 When have you experienced this kind of peace?

Read verses 7-11.

6 For what did Isaiah praise God?

7 Praise is one result of walking with the Lord. What are some evidences that people are walking with God?

8 What are evidences of people not walking with the Lord?

9 Which of these characteristics—positive and negative—are present in your life?

10 What is the purpose of God's judgments?

Read verses 12-19.

11 What do you learn about God from these verses for which to praise Him?

12 How did the people of Judah respond to God's judgment through nations that took them captive?

13 How are people today like the people of Judah?

**We can praise and
be raised
or complain and
remain.**

–joyce meyer

Read verses 20-21.

14 What assurance did God give the remnant of Judah?

15 Why would this assurance elicit praise?

CONSIDER THE MESSAGE

The Bible exhorts us over and over again to offer praise to God. It not only gives us countless examples of praise (most notably in the Psalms, which culminate in a crescendo of praise—see Psalms 148–150), it also commands us to do so (see Hebrews 13:15). But did you ever stop to wonder why? Is God insecure? Does He need us to build Him up? Quite the contrary. God's purpose for praise is twofold: First, God inhabits the praises of His people. As we lift Him up and enthrone Him in our hearts, He makes His home with us. Just as the angels continually declare His praises in heaven, as we declare His praises on earth, we experience a bit of heaven this side of glory. When we praise God, He raises us up to heavenly places in the spiritual realm. There we get a glimpse of who He is and what His larger purposes are.

The opposite of praise is complaining. Just last night I was reading in Exodus about the people of Israel who constantly complained to the point that God actually destroyed some of them in the desert and left the rest wandering around for forty years. As Moses rightly pointed out to them, "You are not grumbling against us, but against the Lord" (Exodus 16:8). All complaining is against God, and He takes it very personally. It's our way of saying, "God, you are not doing a very good job running this universe." I love the way Joyce Meyer puts it: "We can praise and be raised . . . or complain and remain."

No one likes to spend time around whiners and complainers. God is no different. He loves us, but He also knows how much He has done for us. When we start grumbling, He figuratively walks away. And when God walks away, the door is wide open for the devil. It's been said that complaining is like whistling for the devil. If there's one thing Satan loves to hear, it's the complaints of God's people. Read the book of Job, and you'll see that Satan's goal was to get Job to complain against God.

Remember also that there is a war taking place in the heavenlies. When we praise God, we declare that we are on the Lord's side. And let's not give "the accuser of our brothers" (Revelation 12:10) any ammunition when he walks into the presence of God, eager to say, "You've wasted your time pouring out your love on those people. They don't really love you. They're just in it for what they can get. Look how quickly they turn their backs on you the minute everything isn't going their way!" Let's not break God's heart by giving the Enemy just cause to attack His children.

Second, praise builds our faith. The more we recite God's attributes, like His power, glory, and faithfulness, the more confidence we have in Him. What a glorious moment when we can declare from our hearts, "I KNOW whom I have believed, and am PERSUADED that he is able to keep that which I have committed unto him against that day" (2 Timothy 1:12 KJV, emphasis added). Then when life's circumstances begin to shake our confidence, or the devil starts whispering lies in our ears, telling us we can't count on God, we can stand firm. We know better. We won't complain, even in the darkest hour. We will choose to offer the sacrifice of praise.

APPLY THE TRUTH

1 Isaiah could praise God because God's name and renown were the desires of His heart. How important is God's name and renown to you?

2 Do you see the connection between God's reputation in the world and your choice to praise or complain? Explain the connection and your understanding of the importance of praise.

> You don't have to be afraid of praising God too much; unlike humans, He never gets a big head.
>
> –paul dibble

3 Begin a list of everything you know about who God is and what He can do for which you can praise Him. Then spend time praising Him.

4 Memorize Isaiah 26:3–4:

> You will keep in perfect peace
> him whose mind is steadfast,
> because he trusts in you.
> Trust in the Lord forever,
> for the Lord, the Lord, is the Rock eternal.

Session Four
Isaiah 30

God's Faithfulness Gives Us Confidence in Him

SEARCH THE WORD

1 When is it hard for you to place your confidence in God? Why?

Too often we put our confidence in everything and everyone but God, like the people of Judah did. We may claim to place our trust in His faithfulness and loving care, but when trouble comes, we often "take it to the phone instead of taking it to the throne." We can all talk a good talk, and some can even walk a good walk. But the real measure of our faith is where we run to when the going gets tough. Read and meditate on Isaiah 30.

> **I have held many things in my hands, and I have lost them all; but whatever I have placed in God's hands, that I still possess.**
> –martin Luther

Read verses 1-5.

2 When faced with the coming invasion of Assyria, to whom did King Hezekiah and Judah run? (In other words, in whom or what did they place their true confidence?)

3 What did God say would be the outcome of this alliance? Why?

4 What kind of alliances do God's people make with unbelievers today?

5 How is this situation with Judah a warning against such alliances?

Read verses 6-18.

6 How did Isaiah illustrate the futility of the nation's putting its confidence in military might instead of in God?

7 What would be the consequences of the people's turning away from God?

8 In spite of their rebellion, what did God offer His people if they would return to Him as the source of their confidence?

> **Most of us go through life praying a little, planning a little, jockeying for position, hoping, but never being quite certain of anything, and always secretly afraid that we will miss the way. This is a tragic waste of truth and never gives rest to the heart. There is a better way. It is to repudiate our own wisdom and take instead the infinite wisdom of God. Our insistence upon seeing ahead is natural enough, but it is a real hindrance to our spiritual progress.**
>
> –a. w. tozer[1]

9 How can verses 15 and 18 encourage you when you are tempted to put your confidence in other people and things?

Read verses 19–26.

10 What do you learn about God and His faithfulness from these verses?

11 What is significant about this description of God for you today?

Read verses 27-33.

12 How would God deal with Judah's enemies?

13 What encouragement did He offer to those who placed their confidence in Him?

CONSIDER THE MESSAGE

Is life good for you right now? Is it everything you hoped it would be? Do you have every cause for confidence? Or are you in the middle of tough times? Perhaps financial difficulties, marital conflicts, children in trouble? My guess is that you have your share of hardships and heartaches. As a result, on some level, your confidence in God may have been shaken. Like the people of Isaiah's day, you may be tempted to place your confidence in someone or something other than God to resolve your problem. No matter how complex your difficulties, I believe the solution is simple: knowing and trusting in God's faithfulness. The basis of our confidence is the character of God. When we don't know Him, when we have an inaccurate picture of who He is and what He can do, we allow the storms of life to overtake us.

However, as we live our lives before Him, confident that He knows exactly where we are and what needs to be accomplished through our lives, we can walk with joy through confidence in Him. God is always with us. And He's not standing idly by, hoping against hope that life will turn out okay for us. He's active and involved. We can have complete confidence that everything that comes our way has either been sent or allowed by a God who is both all-loving and all-powerful.

However, God is under no obligation to help those who don't turn to Him for help. Isaiah 30 clearly reveals God's displeasure with those who turn elsewhere in their time of need, yet He delights to rescue those who call on His name. I recently heard a powerful illustration of that truth at a women's conference hosted by the Living Word Bible Church in Mesa, Arizona.[2] A man testified before the U.S. Senate that as the R.M.S. *Titanic* was sinking, he was sucked down into a giant air tunnel, expecting at any moment to be swept away. He cried out to God in a prayer rooted in Psalm 91: "He will give his angels charge over me." Instantly, a giant boiler blew up, catapulting the man high into the air, up and away from the doomed ocean liner. He landed in the water just a few feet from a half-full lifeboat.

God had delivered him from a seemingly impossible situation. I don't know what you're facing in your life right now—perhaps you are up against the impossible. We belong to the God of the impossible. A God who loves us, who is greater than our needs and problems, who has the power and ability to help us, who has our best interests in mind. He's a God in whom we can place our confidence at all times!

> **Our confidence in Christ does not make us lazy, negligent or careless, but on the contrary it awakens us, urges us on, and makes us active in living righteous lives and doing good. There is no self-confidence to compare with this.**
> –uLrich zwinqLi

APPLY THE TRUTH

1 What have you learned about God's desires and purposes from this chapter?

2 How can this knowledge help you place your confidence in God instead of in other people and things?

3 How can you increase your confidence in God this week?

4 Memorize Isaiah 30:15 and 21:

> **This is what the Sovereign Lord, the Holy One**
> **of Israel, says: "In repentance and rest is your sal-**
> **vation, in quietness and trust is your strength. . . ."**
> **Whether you turn to the right or to the left,**
> **your ears will hear a voice behind you, saying,**
> **"This is the way; walk in it."**

Session Five
Isaiah 40

God's Faithfulness Is Revealed in His Greatness

SEARCH THE WORD

1 If you had to choose one metaphor to describe God to an unbeliever, what would it be? Why?

Even Isaiah, the prince among the prophets, found it impossible to describe God using just one metaphor. All the word pictures in the universe are inadequate to capture the greatness of our God . . . but no one in history has ever come closer than Isaiah does here in chapter 40. These thirty-one verses are the reason I fell in love with this book.

Read verses 1–8.

2 This chapter begins a turning point in the book of Isaiah. The first thirty-nine chapters deal with God's judgment; the rest of the

book offers comfort. In contrast to the previous judgments and sufferings, what was the good news from the Lord?

3 How did God describe our life here on Earth?

Read verses 9-11.

4 How did Isaiah describe the Lord's coming?

5 What comparison did he use to describe the Lord and His relationship with us?

**God comforts the afflicted...
and afflicts the comfortable.**

6 How does this description affect you?

Read verses 12-17.

7 How did Isaiah describe God's greatness?

> **The great lack of our Christianity today is, we do not *know God*. The answer to every complaint of weakness and failure, the message to every congregation or convention seeking instruction on holiness, should simply be "Where is your God?" If you really believe in God and His power, He will put it right. God is willing and able by His Holy Spirit.**
> –Andrew Murray[1]

8 How do you think Isaiah felt about trying to convey God's wisdom to His people?

9 How does God's power compare with that of the nations?

Read verses 18-20.

10 What did Isaiah say about idols as he rhetorically compared them to God?

Read verses 21-26.

11 Why do you think Isaiah introduced this section on God's transcendence (above all others, including idols and people) with this series of questions?

12 Why can't God be compared to anyone?

13 Why is it important for us to remember this fact?

Read verses 27-31.

14 What complaint did Judah have with God?

If God were small enough for my finite mind to comprehend, He would be very small indeed.

15 How did God answer that complaint?

16 What does God promise those of us who are "tired and weary"?

17 How do you respond to a God like this?

CONSIDER THE MESSAGE

I remember taking my daughter Leah to Disneyland when she was a little girl. When she saw a performer dressed up like Beauty (from *Beauty and the Beast*), she was overjoyed. I thought she was going to leap out of her skin. Now think about it: She could not contain her excitement in the presence of a twenty-something girl dressed up like a fictional, animated character. Do we show equal enthusiasm as we enter the presence of God? Or are we more excited to watch our favorite Thursday night sitcom than we are to keep our daily appointment with God?

If we have to put "daily quiet time" on our little to-do lists, as if the unspeakable privilege of spending time in God's presence is something we need to be reminded of, maybe what we really need is a reminder of just how great this God is—this one who invites us to "approach the throne of grace with confidence, so that we may receive mercy and find grace to help us in our time of need" (Hebrews 4:16). Among other things, I hope you noted the following truths about God's greatness from Isaiah 40:

- His word stands forever.
- He is the Sovereign Lord, who comes with power.
- His right arm rules for Him.
- He has a reward in store for us.
- He tends His flock like a shepherd.
- He cannot be measured but instead measures all things.
- His mind is far beyond our comprehension.
- Even mighty nations are like a drop in a bucket compared to Him.
- He is incomparable. Compared to Him, all the people of the earth are like grasshoppers.
- He sits enthroned above the earth.
- The entire universe is like a little pitch-tent for Him.
- He rules over the rulers of this world.
- He is Creator and Sustainer of the entire universe.
- He is great in power, mighty in strength.
- He is the Everlasting God.
- He never grows tired or weary.
- Those who wait on Him will soar on wings like eagles.

Wow! If you knew a human being with a fraction of that power and influence and he told you to "stop by anytime and ask for whatever you need," do you think you'd need someone to remind you to take him up on the offer? I don't think so!

Last week I visited the Hearst Castle on the central California coast. This is the magnificent estate where William Randolph Hearst once entertained dignitaries and celebrities from around the world. You can bet the moment he issued an invitation, people were packing their bags, clamoring for the chance to sit at his banquet table. I know I sure would have jumped at the chance. Our God is so much greater than Mr. Hearst, even at the height of his worldly power.

Isn't it amazing to know that we have such a mighty God? Not only is He faithful, He backs up that faithfulness with His greatness. What good is a true friend who has no strength to help you when the chips are down? God not only loves us, He is able by His power to address our every need.

APPLY THE TRUTH

> **When you behold the greatness of God, then you will see everything else in life in its proper perspective.**
> –warren w. wiersbe

1 What did you learn about God's greatness from this passage that is significant for you right now?

2 Spend some time praising God for His greatness, focusing especially on the truths you listed above.

3 Select one of the above truths to focus on this week. Choose a verse from this chapter about that truth to memorize and meditate on, and write it on an index card to carry with you while you're learning it.

4 Also memorize Isaiah 40:29–31:

> He gives strength to the weary
> and increases the power of the weak.
> Even youths grow tired and weary,
> and young men stumble and fall;
> but those who hope in the LORD
> will renew their strength.
> They will soar on wings like eagles;
> they will run and not grow weary,
> they will walk and not be faint.

Session Six
Isaiah 45

God's Faithfulness Transforms Us Into Vessels He Can Use

SEARCH THE WORD

1 If someone were going to introduce you to a group, what three words or phrases would that person use to describe you, other than your job title?

How people are introduced gives an impression about who they are and what they are like. When God introduces people He chooses descriptions that are meaningful to His audience as evidenced in Isaiah 45. Read and meditate on this chapter.

Read verses 1–7.

2 Even before Cyrus was born, God mentioned that pagan king of Persia in Isaiah's prophecies. Why did God call Cyrus "His anointed"?

3 What was God's word to Cyrus?

> As truly as God by His power once
> created all things, so by that same
> power must God every moment
> maintain all things. We as His
> creatures have not only to look back
> to the origin and beginning of our
> existence and acknowledge that we
> owe everything to God—our chief
> care, His highest virtue, and only
> happiness, now and through all
> eternity—but we must also present
> ourselves as empty vessels, in which
> God can dwell and manifest His
> power and goodness.
>
> —andrew murray[1]

4 What part would God play in his actions?

5 How did God stress His own uniqueness?

6 What else do you learn about God from these verses?

Read verses 8-10.

7 God reassures His people that a better time is coming. How did He describe it?

8 Then He brought their attention to their relationship with Him. What does this description of people as clay and God as the Potter tell us about ourselves and about God?

9 Why is it useless to argue with God?

10 So why do we do it anyway?

> We honor God by choosing to trust Him when we don't understand what He is doing or why He has allowed some adverse circumstance to occur. As we seek God's glory, we may be sure that He has purposed our good and that He will not be frustrated in fulfilling that purpose.
> —jerry bridges[2]

Read verses 11-13.

11 Why did God warn the people against questioning His use of Cyrus?

12 God put Cyrus in a position of authority to accomplish His purposes. What were they?

Read verses 14-19.

13 How will the surrounding nations change in the future?

14 How will they acknowledge God's uniqueness?

Read verses 20-25.

15 What was God's appeal to the Gentile nations? Why?

16 What will happen to those who "have raged against" the Lord?

17 In contrast, how will Israel's descendants be found righteous?

CONSIDER THE MESSAGE

Over and over God said, "I am the Lord, and there is no other." With a description like that, you'd think we'd all bow down and obey Him without questioning. But in reality, we fight with Him all the time.

Have you ever stopped to think that every time you compare yourself to someone else, you are quarreling with your Maker? You are saying, "God, you really messed up this time. You didn't make me the right way. You should have made me like so-and-so." Yet Psalm 139 and many other passages clearly demonstrate that God deliberately and carefully created you exactly the way you are. He made you to serve and glorify Him in a way that no one else can. He gave you a unique set of talents, physical characteristics, emotional makeup, temperament, and life experiences for a specific reason. Until the day you fully accept the package God rolled together when He created you, you will never become the person He intended you to be.

When you pursue a ministry God didn't create you to fulfill— or undertake any project He hasn't called you to do—you are quarreling with your Maker. You're saying, "God, I've got a better idea than you do. I know better than you what needs to be done around this church. I know better than you do what needs to be accomplished through my life."

Just as the potter fashions a beautiful, delicate vase to grace the table and a sturdy pot to boil water, God makes different people to fulfill different purposes. There's no factory in heaven; each of us is unique. God made you exactly the way He did because He has a specific purpose He wants you to fulfill, just like He had for Cyrus.

I had a friend in college who was an art student. I remember watching him work with the potter's wheel. One day he let me take a shot at it. I'm a cocky kind of person, so I figured it would be easy. I thought I'd just stroll on over, give the wheel a few spins, and voila! a beautiful vase. I expected the clay to be soft and easy to mold, like glorified Play-Doh. But it wasn't like that at all. The clay was incredibly heavy. When the wheel was spinning around, I couldn't do anything with the clay. I couldn't believe how hard it was to push and shove. The clay and the force of gravity constantly fought against me. I tried to push it in one direction, and it went in the other. That ugly, smelly pile of clay absolutely refused to cooperate.

Sometimes my friend would spend hours working with a pile of clay. He'd finally mold it into a beautiful, nearly complete form. And suddenly the whole thing would collapse. He'd have no choice but to smash it and start the work all over again. That is, if it hadn't already been reduced to junk-pile material.

The Bible says we're like that pile of clay. Oh, how much easier our lives would be if only we would cooperate! How much faster we would be transformed into a useful vessel if only we would stay centered and remain moldable in the Potter's hands.

What do you quarrel with God about? Could it be the very thing God wants to use as a ministry to others? Do you fight against the Potter? Do you fuss and squirm and protest every time He tries to make adjustments in your life? Do you collapse when He attempts major changes? Wouldn't your life be much better if you simply cooperated with God's work in your life? So often I pray, "Lord, let me hear it from your lips so I don't have to learn it the hard way—from life." Some lessons, though, can only be learned the hard way. In those cases I pray, "Lord, help me get the lesson right the first time so I don't have to suffer through it again!"

How about you? Will you resolve to remain moldable? Will you decide today to cooperate with the Potter as He seeks to form you into a vessel He can use?[3]

APPLY THE TRUTH

Don't bother to give God instructions, just report for duty.
–corrie ten boom

1 What kind of lump of clay have you been on the Potter's wheel?

2 What changes do you need to make so God can more easily mold you into a usable vessel for His purposes?

3 Which change will you work on this week? Write an action plan for doing so.

4 Memorize Isaiah 45:9:

> **Woe to him who quarrels
> with his Maker,
> to him who is but a potsherd
> among the potsherds on the ground.
> Does the clay say to the potter,
> "What are you making?"
> Does your work say,
> "He has no hands"?**

Session Seven
Isaiah 46

God's Faithfulness Enables Us to Overcome Our Dependence on Idols

SEARCH THE WORD

1 When do you feel burdened and overwhelmed? Why?

Life holds a profound irony: anything we lift up will ultimately bring us down. Whether it's money, personal appearance, physical fitness, status, or even marriage and family, if it becomes more important in our lives than God, it is an idol . . . and God will surely knock it down as He explained in Isaiah 46. Read and meditate on this chapter.

Read verses 1-2.

2 How did Isaiah describe the gods the Babylonians worshiped?

3 How do you know they are helpless?

4 What will happen to them?

Read verses 3-4.

5 In contrast to these idols, what does God offer His people?

6 What about God's offer appeals most to you?

Whatever or whoever you think about most is your idol.
–don staen

Read verses 5-7.

7 How is God different from these idols?

8 What type of idols do people worship today?

9 How have they failed those who worship them?

Read verses 8-13.

10 What did God command His people to do? Why?

11 How did He describe His people?

12 What will God accomplish? How?

13 What do you learn about God's character and faithfulness from this passage?

> You don't have to go to heathen lands today to find false gods. America is full of them. Whatever you love more than God is your idol.
>
> —d. L. moody

CONSIDER THE MESSAGE

In describing the Israelites, Isaiah said they were burdened down by the idols, or images, they carried around. Although we don't think of ourselves as idol worshipers, is it possible that you are carrying images that are burdening you down? Perhaps they are images of the way you think life should be: more precisely, images of what you think your lifestyle should be.

I meet many people who are enslaved to their images of the great American lifestyle. And those images have indeed become a burden for the weary:

- A college degree, preferably from a prestigious school.
- A 2,500-square-foot professionally decorated house with a two-car garage, in the right neighborhood.
- Dinner out at least once a week.
- Professional haircuts, acrylic nails, full salon treatments.
- Weekly maid service.
- Great vacations every year, including Hawaii and Europe.
- Latest computer and accessories.
- Latest home theater components.
- New car every two or three years.
- Well-dressed kids—in store-bought clothes. Wal-Mart clothes, however, don't cut it. Sneakers matter most. Your kids need at least thirty sets of clothes to be normal.
- Your kids involved in sports. Fortunately there's a sport for every season. (I once read a magazine article describing the American obsession with children's sports. The writer quipped, "The Cold War is over . . . and the East Germans won!" If children's sporting events are the central focus of your household, you might pray over the truth of those words.)

We're burdened down by images like these. All the stuff we accumulate, the status quo we pursue, becomes a burden for the weary. We need two incomes to keep up, so either Mom has to work or Dad has to work longer hours. It doesn't have to be that way. We don't have to live in bondage to the status quo. Money, possessions, and conformity cannot deliver us, as Isaiah stated: "Though one cries out to it [riches and man-made idols], it does not answer; it cannot save him from his troubles" (Isaiah 46:7b).

> Come to me, all you who are weary and burdened, and I will give you rest. Take my yoke upon you and learn from me, for I am gentle and humble in heart, and you will find rest for your souls. For my yoke is easy and my burden is light.
>
> –jesus christ (matthew 11:28-30)

The only one we can cry out to for deliverance is God. The only one who can save us from our troubles is God: "I am he, I am he who will sustain you. I have made you and I will carry you; I will sustain you and I will rescue you" (Isaiah 46:4).

God can deliver us, He can rescue us, but we have to be willing to be rescued.[1]

APPLY THE TRUTH

1 What kind of self-imposed burdens and/or idols are you carrying around that have taken God's place in your life?

2 What do you need to do to get rid of them?

How will you start this week?

3 How can you remember God's faithfulness to you as you give up these burdens and idols?

4 Memorize Isaiah 46:4:

> **Even to your old age and gray hairs I am he,**
> **I am he who will sustain you.**
> **I have made you and I will carry you;**
> **I will sustain you and I will rescue you.**

Session Eight

Isaiah 51

God's Faithfulness Endures Forever

SEARCH THE WORD

1 Have you ever had someone in your life whom you considered an enemy? What was the outcome of that situation?

Just like the people of Isaiah's day, we have both human enemies and a powerful Enemy seeking to destroy us. But God's faithfulness enables us to secure victory over both human and spiritual enemies as we learn to overcome evil with good. Read and meditate on Isaiah 51.

Read verses 1–3.

2 What did the Lord tell the believing remnant in Babylon to look back to? Why?

3 How were Abraham and Sarah a rock?

4 What does the future restoration of Israel tell us about God?

Read verses 4-8.

5 What was ahead for God's people in exile?

6 Why did God tell them not to be afraid?

7 What do you learn about God's justice from these verses?

8 How have you recently experienced God's faithfulness with regard to overcoming enemies?

Read verses 9-11.

9 For what did Isaiah ask God?

10 Why did Isaiah mention the historical event of the Exodus from Egypt?

Read verses 12-16.

11 What comfort did the Lord offer His people as an answer to their prayer?

12 What do you learn about God's faithfulness from this answer?

Read verses 17-23.

13 What happened to the people because of their disobedience?

> God wants us to
> be victors, not
> victims; to grow,
> not grovel; to
> soar, not sink; to
> overcome, not to
> be overwhelmed.
> –wiLLiam a. ward

14 How does our disobedience affect our lives?

CONSIDER THE MESSAGE

Throughout history, God's people have always been surrounded by enemies on every side. Yet whenever they trusted Him, God proved faithful. He fought on their behalf and overcame their enemies—often without their having to lift a finger. As Isaiah reminds them in today's passage, God wiped out the Egyptians in the Red Sea. Under Gideon's leadership, God enabled three hundred men to scatter the entire Midianite army simply by blowing trumpets and breaking jars of clay (Judges 7). During the reign of King Jehoshaphat of Judah, "as they began to sing and praise, the Lord set ambushes against the men of Ammon and Moab and Mount Seir who were invading Judah, and they were defeated. . . . When the men of Judah came to the place that overlooks the desert and looked toward the vast army, they saw only dead bodies lying on the ground; no one had escaped" (2 Chronicles 20:22, 24).

In response to the prayers of King Hezekiah, God destroyed the Assyrian army of Sennacherib while they slept in their tents (2 Kings 18–19; 2 Chronicles 32). They had been poised to invade Judah after conquering Israel. Here's how Lord Byron described it in his famous poem "The Destruction of Sennacherib," first published in 1815.

The Assyrian came down like the wolf on the fold,
And his cohorts were gleaming in purple and gold;
And the sheen of their spears was like stars on the sea,
When the blue wave rolls nightly on deep Galilee.

Like the leaves of the forest when Summer is green,
That host with their banners at sunset were seen:
Like the leaves of the forest when Autumn hath blown,
That host on the morrow lay withered and strown.

For the Angel of Death spread his wings on the blast,
And breathed in the face of the foe as he passed;
And the eyes of the sleepers waxed deadly and chill,
And their hearts but once heaved, and for ever grew still!

And there lay the steed with his nostril all wide,
But through it there rolled not the breath of his pride;
And the foam of his gasping lay white on the turf,
And cold as the spray of the rock-beating surf.

And there lay the rider distorted and pale,
With the dew on his brow, and the rust on his mail:
And the tents were all silent, the banners alone,
The lances unlifted, the trumpet unblown.

And the widows of Ashur are loud in their wail,
And the idols are broke in the temple of Baal;
And the might of the Gentile, unsmote by the sword,
Hath melted like snow in the glance of the Lord!

God is well aware of your enemies and your Enemy, who is no doubt the driving force behind every battle waged against you. God's Word tells us exactly how to handle both adversaries. In the first instance, Jesus instructs us to love our enemies and pray for those who persecute us (Matthew 5:44). In the book of Romans, we are warned not to be overcome with evil, but to "overcome evil with good" (12:21). God wants to fight your battle for you, just as He did for King Jehoshaphat, whom he told, "You will not have to fight this battle. Take up your positions; stand firm and see the deliverance the Lord will give you" (2 Chronicles 20:17). Is it possible that the only reason God has not yet overcome your enemies is because you're still standing in His way? Rather than thinking about revenge, fill your mind with thoughts of praise for your faithful God.

As for the Enemy of your soul, Jesus set an example. He defeated him, time after time, with three simple words: "It is written" (Matthew 4:4, 7, and 10). We would do well to remember that we are being attacked by a defeated enemy. Of course, that also makes him desperate and, therefore, very dangerous. As Revelation

12:12 reminds us, "He is filled with fury, because he knows that his time is short." Yet the day is coming when he too will bend the knee before our God and King. To borrow a teenage phrase, "He ain't all that." Just as God defeated the enemies of His people through the Old Testament, He has done the same for us. He is faithful!

APPLY THE TRUTH

1 As you studied this chapter, what struck you most about God's faithfulness in overcoming the enemies of His people?

2 How have you experienced this overcoming power recently?

3 Spend time praising God for His faithfulness and what it means to you.

4 Memorize Isaiah 51:6–7:

> But my salvation will last forever,
> my righteousness will never fail.
> Hear me, you who know what is right,
> you people who have my law in your hearts:
> Do not fear the reproach of men
> or be terrified by their insults.

God's Faithfulness Gave Us a Savior

SEARCH THE WORD

1 When have you needed rescuing?

How did you get out of that situation?

We're painfully aware of our need for a rescuer in situations such as financial trouble, problems with a spouse or kids, being buried with work, loneliness, a major fight with a friend, or an illness. We secretly hope a white knight will come dashing through the door and everything will be all right. But getting delivered from sin isn't usually on the felt-need list, although it's more critical than any of these other situations. Read and meditate on Isaiah 52:13–53:12.

Read 52:13-15.

2 It's not hard to figure out that God's servant in this passage is Jesus, the promised Messiah. How did God describe His actions and appearance?

3 How would people respond to Him? Why?

Nothing was accidental about the cross of Christ. The Son of God was not suddenly overcome by the wickedness of man and nailed to a cross. Quite the contrary, the cross was the means by which the Son of God overcame the wickedness of man. To secure the keys to the house of David and open the door of salvation to all who would enter, God drove His Son like a nail in a sure place. A firm place. An enduring place.

–beth moore[1]

Read 53:1-3.

4 Why do you think people wouldn't believe this message about God's way of deliverance from our sins?

5 How did God further describe His servant?

6 How would He be treated?

7 How did Jesus fulfill these prophecies?

Read 53:4-6.

8 What would the Messiah's suffering accomplish for believers?

9 How did Isaiah describe us?

10 How well does this description fit you?

> Why is the cross the symbol of our faith? To find the answer look no farther than the cross itself. Its design couldn't be simpler. One beam horizontal—the other vertical. One reaches out—like God's love. The other reaches up—as does God's holiness. One represents the width of his love; the other reflects the height of his holiness. The cross is the intersection. The cross is where God forgave his children without lowering his standards.
>
> —max Lucado[2]

11 What would God do with our sin? Why?

Read 53:7-9.

12 How would the Messiah react to the suffering men would inflict on Him? Why?

13 How would His death contradict His life?

Read 53:10-12.

14 What was the Lord's will for His Son?

15 How would Jesus "be satisfied" after His death for our sins?

16 Summarize the reasons for Jesus' death on the cross.

CONSIDER THE MESSAGE

Every one of us, as followers of Jesus Christ, has a testimony— a moment or a season in our life when we recognized our need for a Savior. Granted, some of us have more dramatic conversion stories than others, but the angels in heaven throw the exact same party whenever *anyone* receives Christ as Savior. As I often tell people raised in Christian homes, they certainly do have a testimony—it's a testimony of God's faithfulness to their families. No family moves from the kingdom of darkness into the kingdom of His blessed light without someone, somewhere, taking a stand for righteousness. Maybe it was your great-grandmother or your great-great-grandfather. Don't apologize for that! Don't mumble, "Oh, I don't have a testimony . . . I was just raised in a Christian home," as if that's something to be ashamed of. Be grateful that you received the greatest gift any parents can pass on to their children: a spiritual inheritance. Isn't that what we want for our children? Then why be sorry your parents gave it to you? Rejoice that you encountered the Savior, whenever and however you did!

I'm one of those with a mess-timony. Oops. I mean, testimony. I freely admit that when God tracked me down and dragged me kicking and screaming into the kingdom of heaven, I was not only a drug addict, I was also a drug dealer. I was so enslaved to drugs that I would actually give kids free drugs just to get them hooked and land a long-term customer.

But I praise God because He did not leave me in that place. In July 1980 I received a phone call from a high-school friend who invited me to go on vacation in northern Pennsylvania. He said the setting was breathtaking and the people were fabulous. He concluded the conversation by saying, "I'm paying your way, so you can't say no. I'm picking you up tomorrow at 5:00 A.M."

I hung up the phone and figured, *Hey, what have I got to lose? It's a free vacation.* I quickly packed my bags, including my string bikini and a couple of joints (that's marijuana cigarettes, for the uninitiated). Was I in for a big surprise when we pulled into the Lutheran Brethren Retreat Center. Of course, I wasn't nearly as surprised as the camp directors were when they

> Man does, indeed, need a radical change of heart; he needs to begin to hate his sin instead of loving it, and to love God instead of hating him; he needs, in a word, to be reconciled to God. And the place, above all others, where this change takes place is at the foot of the cross, when he apprehends something of the hatred of God for sin and his indescribable love for the sinner.
>
> –j. n. d. anderson[3]

saw me! Nevertheless, the leaders clearly explained to me my desperate need for a Savior. And because Christ died for my sins, I could be forgiven and spend eternity with God.

On the third day of the conference, I was sitting on the bank of the Delaware River when it suddenly became real to me: Even if I were the only person on the planet, Jesus Christ would have gone to the cross to pay the price for my sins. He would have endured all the suffering Isaiah described in this passage just for me. And He would have endured it just for you too. If you have embraced the promised Messiah as your Savior, I rejoice with you. If not, I urge you to prayerfully consider your own need for a Savior.[4]

APPLY THE TRUTH

1 How has Jesus' death changed your life? Share the story of your salvation.

2 Praise God for His love and faithfulness that caused Him to send His Son to the cross to be the Savior for your sin.

3 Memorize Isaiah 53:5–6:

> **But he was pierced for our transgressions,**
> **he was crushed for our iniquities;**
> **the punishment that brought us peace**
> **was upon him,**
> **and by his wounds we are healed.**
> **We all, like sheep, have gone astray,**
> **each of us has turned to his own way;**
> **and the Lord has laid on him**
> **the iniquity of us all.**

Session Ten

Isaiah 55

God's Faithfulness Satisfies Our Deepest Needs

SEARCH THE WORD

1 When do you feel satisfied? Why?

If you're honest, you'll admit there are times—perhaps too many—when people and things leave you feeling empty. Fortunately, God promises to satisfy the deepest needs of our hearts, as explained in Isaiah 55. Read and meditate on this chapter.

Read verses 1-5.

2 What invitation does God extend?

3 What does "coming to God" mean?

4 How did God describe the people to whom He issued this invitation?

5 Why do we go looking for satisfaction in all the wrong places rather than in God?

6 What did God promise to those who accept His invitation to come?

> There is a God-shaped
> vacuum in the heart of every
> man which cannot be filled
> by any created thing,
> but only by God the Creator
> made known through
> Jesus Christ.
> –bLaise pascaL

Read verses 6-13.

7 What does God urge people to do, and what will He do for them in return?

8 What are some specific ways we can obey these commands today?

9 What time limit does God give us?

10 How do God's thoughts and ways differ from ours?

11 How does verse 10 illustrate the effectiveness of God's Word?

12 How can we work with God to get His Word out?

**My people have committed
two sins: They have forsaken
me, the spring
of living water, and have
dug their own cisterns,
broken cisterns that cannot
hold water.**

–jeremiah 2:13

13 How does Isaiah compare nature to the ways of God and the Word of God?

14 When and how has nature reminded you of God and what He can do?

CONSIDER THE MESSAGE

I firmly believe God deliberately designed all human beings with a hole in our hearts the size of the Grand Canyon. It's what Blaise Pascal termed the "God-shaped vacuum"—a place that can only be filled through a personal relationship with our Creator. All of us sense that emptiness within, and we are driven to fill it. But rather than turning to God for fulfillment, as we should, many of us run everywhere else instead and try to buy satisfaction in a myriad of ways.

We go out into the world with a little clamoring bucket, and we hand it to the people around us and say, "Fill me. Fix me. Love me. Make me feel okay." We turn to our parents, our spouses, our children, our friends, our churches, our careers, expecting them to be to us what only God can be. We fill our lives with stuff—and more stuff, often spending money we can't afford to spend. The result is what I've termed Da Bucket Lady Syndrome.

Da Bucket Lady always thinks the answer to her emptiness is right around the next corner. So she tries to get her bucket filled with accomplishments and material things. She tries to fill it with the perfect house and the perfect circle of friends. Da Bucket Lady might even look good because she has to have great clothes, the right hairstyle, and expensive makeup. She's busy at church, trying to fill her bucket with Christian rituals and religious busywork. The reality is she will never rest until that hole is filled . . . and it can never be filled with a bucket. Isaiah put it this way: "Why spend money on what is not bread, and your labor on what does not satisfy?" (55:2).

A perfect example is the Samaritan woman who met Jesus at a well. (You can read her story in John 4:4–42.) This Bucket Lady had five husbands, plus she was living with another guy, and we can only imagine how many boyfriends were thrown into the mix. Talk about looking for satisfaction in all the wrong people. You would think that if it were possible for a man to fill a woman's bucket, one of these men would have gotten it right if only by accident. I mean, at some point, wouldn't the law of averages have worked in her favor?

The problem is, it's not possible.

So she met up with Jesus. And He told her the same thing He tells the rest of us Bucket Ladies: "Everyone who drinks this water will be thirsty again, but whoever drinks the water I give him will never thirst. Indeed, the water I give him will become in him a spring of water welling up to eternal life" (John 4:13–14).

Then the story includes a fascinating detail: "Then, leaving her water jar . . ." (v. 28).

Did you catch that? She left her bucket at the well!

Once she allowed Jesus to fill that hole in her heart, to place within her that spring of water welling up to eternal life, she didn't need her bucket anymore. She didn't have to live like a Bucket Lady anymore. You don't either.

God himself can fill your heart. He can satisfy your deepest needs—if you'll let Him.[1]

APPLY THE TRUTH

1 What are some things you turn to in an attempt to fill the God-shaped vacuum in your life?

God sends no one away empty except those who are full of themselves.
–dwight L. moody

2 Why do you turn to these instead of to the One who can truly satisfy you?

3 What will you do to say yes to God instead?

4 Memorize Isaiah 55:10–11:

> As the rain and the snow
> come down from heaven,
> and do not return to it
> without watering the earth
> and making it bud and flourish,
> so that it yields seed for the sower
> and bread for the eater,
> so is my word that goes out from my mouth:
> It will not return to me empty,
> but will accomplish what I desire
> and achieve the purpose for which I sent it.

Session Eleven
Isaiah 58

God's Faithfulness Guides Us

SEARCH THE WORD

1 Describe a time when you knew God was guiding you.

God promises to guide us, but He expects certain behavior from us as a prerequisite for that guidance, as Isaiah explained in this passage. Read and meditate on Isaiah 58.

Read verses 1–5.

2 How did God's people go through the motions of worshiping Him?

3 How did their fasting prevent them from receiving God's guidance?

4 How accurately do these verses describe God's people today? Explain your answer.

Read verses 6-12.

> True worship is
> **not lip service but**
> **life service.**
> –anonymous

5 In contrast to the people's behavior, what kind of fasting did God want?

6 What might a heart-driven fast look like today?

7 What rewards did God promise for this kind of fasting?

8 What kind of behavior does God expect from His people before He guides them?

9 How does God guide people who are in right relationship with Him?

Read verses 13-14.

10 Since we are no longer under Old Testament law, the Sabbath has a different meaning for us. (See Matthew 12:1–13; Colossians 2:16–23; Hebrews 4:1–11.) Christ himself is our rest. Nevertheless, it remains a good principle to set aside one day each week to rest from your ordinary routine and focus on your relationship with God. How might this prove beneficial?

CONSIDER THE MESSAGE

I live in Arizona, so I know about sun-scorched land and desert places inhabited only by rattlesnakes and Gila monsters. In the desert, there are no landmarks to guide you. Everything looks the same. A cactus is a cactus. You could go in circles for miles and never know it. Then again, you could be making tremendous progress, even though it feels like you're going in circles.

> **When you take control of your physical appetite [through the discipline of fasting], you develop strength to take control of your emotional appetite.**
> –eLmer towns

Even in desert places, God has said He will guide us and satisfy our needs. One way to listen more intently for that guidance is by setting aside a time each day to rest from the cares of this world. The ideal way to incorporate such a spiritual discipline (and, yes, it is a discipline) is to commit yourself to a daily quiet time, devoted to Bible study and prayer. Then add times of extended prayer, study, and meditation one day per week. If such a Sabbath is honored from your heart rather than out of a sense of duty or as a religious ritual, it can be a tremendous blessing. That blessing is multiplied when you incorporate fasting. Nothing unstops your ears like the silence of your formerly-constantly-munching lips!

I wish I could tell you that if you take time for spiritual disciplines, you'll never get lost again along your spiritual journey. I wish

I could tell you that every day for the rest of your life you'll leap out of bed, eager to spend a quiet time with the Lord, and your first fast will last forty days, culminating in a vision of heaven. To be honest, I have heard people report having had that experience. However, I suspect that most of you, at some point along your spiritual journey, will go through a sun-scorched place. A place where it feels like no spiritual progress is being made. That's when you'll have to make a choice. Will you allow God to guide you forward? Or will you turn back?

Anyone can follow God when the following is easy, but God offers a promise to those who continue following even when it's tough. God says He will strengthen you and make you like a well-watered garden. In other words, He'll give you what you need to grow.

Yet He goes one step further. Not only will you experience personal growth, but God will also enable you to make a difference in the lives of others. You will rebuild ancient ruins—repairing the fallout of problems that may have plagued your family for generations. You'll provide a new, solid foundation for your children to build on after you.

God will even enable you to make a difference in your community as you become a "Repairer of Broken Walls" and the "Restorer of Streets." That means you'll be an agent of security and peace, a haven of rest for the weary. As you stand firm, you'll discover that people will come to you in their times of crisis. You, in turn, can point them to the only One who can guide them through a sun-scorched land.[1]

APPLY THE TRUTH

1 What changes do you need to make in your worship and behavior so God *can* guide you?

2 Choose one change to work on this week, and write an action plan.

3 How can you honor God on Sundays or another day set aside for worship?

> **The life of the believer is a conducted tour, and the skillful guide is Abraham's guide and ours. He knows the end of the journey, which is in view, and he knows the best way to arrive there.**
>
> –fred mitcheLL

4 How might you incorporate principles of the Sabbath rest into your daily routine? How might you do so in a more focused way, once each week?

5 Memorize Isaiah 58:11:

> **The Lord will guide you always;**
> **he will satisfy your needs in a**
> **sun-scorched land**
> **and will strengthen your frame.**
> **You will be like a well-watered garden,**
> **like a spring whose waters never fail.**

Session Twelve
Isaiah 62

God's Faithfulness Chooses Us and Delights in Us

SEARCH THE WORD

1 When has someone specifically chosen you for something? How did you feel?

We all want to be chosen—instead of ignored or rejected—whether it's as a friend, a team member, a spouse, a contest winner, etc. Isn't it wonderful to know that God chose you before the foundation of the world? Not only that, He has a great reward in store for you. Read and meditate on Isaiah 62.

> **For he chose us in him before the creation of the world to be holy and blameless in his sight.**
> –ephesians 1:4

Read verses 1-5.

2 Even though He had chosen the Israelites as His people, why didn't the Lord remain silent about their sin and judgment?

3 What changes did He predict for His chosen people and for Zion in the coming kingdom?

4 What is significant about the city being "called by a new name"? (Hephzibah means "my delight is in her," and Beulah means "married.")

5 When does God "take delight in" and "rejoice over" us?

Read verses 6–9.

6 How are those who pray for Jerusalem like watchmen on the walls?

7 What do you learn about prayer from these verses?

8 What does God promise His people?

9 How will these promises change their lives?

God's promises are like the stars; the darker the night, the brighter they shine.
–david nicholas

Read verses 10-12.

10 What are God's people to do as they wait for their Savior, Messiah Jesus?

11 How might these commands affect the hearers?

12 What is significant about each new name God will give His people and Jerusalem?

13 How does God show His faithfulness in choosing and seeking after people?

CONSIDER THE MESSAGE

Congratulations! You have come to the final chapter in our study of Isaiah. What an awesome accomplishment! And there is no better place to conclude than with the realization that, someday, Jesus is coming back for us. Not only has He opened the door for us to enjoy many spiritual blessings in this life, He has given us the Holy Spirit as a deposit, guaranteeing our place in eternity with him (2 Corinthians 1:22). The Christian walk is an exciting adventure, and there's no other approach to this world that makes any sense to me. I'm glad God chose me to be His daughter and am grateful for the many benefits that title bestows upon me. But as the apostle Paul put it, "If only for this life we have hope in Christ, we are to be pitied more than all men" (1 Corinthians 15:19).

There's more to human existence than living and dying—even more than enjoying the abundant life Jesus promises us as believers (John 10:10). While it's possible for us to experience a bit of heaven here on earth—moments when our fellowship with God is sweet, poignant times with our families, or even that simple bliss that comes from eating an ice cream sundae on a perfect summer day—we are not home yet, friends. There is more, so much more, in store for us. And Isaiah gives us an incredible glimpse of what that coming kingdom will be like. Someday, Jesus will establish His eternal kingdom. And we who have followed Him will be rewarded for our faithfulness. Indeed, the Bible says we will reign with God throughout all eternity and our place in that kingdom will be determined by how faithful we are in this life.

Remember that the next time you are tempted to do the bare minimum in your walk with God. Don't rob yourself of a future blessing! Instead, store up your treasures in heaven (Matthew 6:

19–20). Even now, Jesus is preparing a place for you. If that were not so, He would have told us (John 14:2–3). Jesus is coming back, and He's bringing our reward with Him. Oh, how we should long for that glorious day! How different our lives would be if we could grab hold of the vision Isaiah imparted and make it our own.

I pray that our journey together has been a blessing and that you have learned for yourself how to "extract the precious" from God's precious Word. I hope you will always treasure those moments during the study when God tutored you, one-on-one. Treasure the truths you have gleaned and the skills you have attained. They are priceless possessions, yet no one can ever steal them from you. Until our paths cross again, I leave you with a psalm of praise to our great King. Amen! Come, Lord Jesus!

Praise the Lord.
Praise the Lord from the heavens,
praise him in the heights above.
Praise him, all his angels,
praise him, all his heavenly hosts.
Praise him, sun and moon,
Praise him, you highest heavens
and you waters above the skies.
Let them praise the name of the Lord,
for he commanded and they were created.
He set them in place for ever and ever;
he gave a decree that will never pass away.
Praise the Lord from the earth,
you great sea creatures and all ocean depths,
lightning and hail, snow and clouds,
you mountains and all hills,
fruit trees and all cedars,
wild animals and all cattle,
small creatures and flying birds,
kings of the earth and all nations,
you princes and all rulers on earth,
young men and maidens,

old men and children.
Let them praise the name of the Lord,
for his name alone is exalted;
his splendor is above the earth and the heavens.
He has raised up for his people a horn,
the praise of all his saints,
of Israel, the people close to his heart.
Praise the Lord. (Psalm 148)

APPLY THE TRUTH

1 How can knowing that God personally chose you change your thoughts, attitudes, and actions?

2 How can you live out one of those changes this week? Develop a practical, specific action plan.

3 Memorize Isaiah 62:11–12:

> **The Lord has made proclamation**
> **to the ends of the earth:**
> **"Say to the Daughter of Zion,**
> **'See, your Savior comes!**
> **See, his reward is with him,**
> **and his recompense accompanies him.'"**
> **They will be called the Holy People,**
> **the Redeemed of the Lord;**
> **and you will be called Sought After,**
> **the City No Longer Deserted.**

Leader's Guide

TO ENCOURAGE GROUP DISCUSSION

- If your group isn't used to discussing together, explain at the beginning of the first session that these studies are designed for discussion, not lecture. Encourage each member to participate, but keep in mind that it may take several meetings before shy members feel comfortable enough to participate.
- Encourage discussion by asking several people to contribute answers to a question. "What do the rest of you think?" or "Is there anything else that could be added?" are two ways of doing so.
- Receive all contributions warmly. Never bluntly reject what anyone says, even if you think the answer is incorrect. Instead, ask what others think and/or ask the person to identify the verse(s) that led her to that conclusion.
- Be sure you don't talk too much as the leader. Redirect questions that you are asked. A discussion should move in the form of a bouncing ball, back and forth between members, not in the form of a fan with the discussion always coming back to the leader at the point. The leader acts as a moderator. As members of a group get to know one another better, the discussion will move more freely.
- Don't be afraid of pauses or long silences. People need time to think about the questions. Never answer your own question— either rephrase it or move on to another area for discussion.
- Watch hesitant members for an indication by facial expression or body language that they have something to say, and then give them an encouraging nod or speak their names.
- Discourage too-talkative members from monopolizing the discussion by specifically directing questions to others. If necessary,

speak to them privately about the need for discussion and enlist their help in encouraging everyone to participate.

* End the sessions by praying for one another, thanking God for growth, and asking Him for help to practice the truth discovered during the week. Vary the prayer times by staying together, breaking into smaller groups or pairs, using sentence prayers, etc. Resist the ever-present temptation to spend more time talking about prayer than actually praying. When it's time to pray, don't waste time on elaborate prayer requests for Susie's uncle's cousin's neighbor's grandmother. Instead, allow the Holy Spirit to bring forth what is on His heart as He prompts individual members to pray.

DISCUSSION LEADER'S NOTES

1: GOD'S FAITHFULNESS DELIVERS US FROM HYPOCRISY: ISAIAH 1

Purpose: To evaluate our lives for religious hypocrisy and take steps to bring our hearts and actions in line with what pleases God.

Question 1: Each study begins with an icebreaker question like this one. Ask a few volunteers to share their answers. As your group members get to know one another better, you may want to go around the circle and have everyone respond to this opening question. Pray for sensitivity in how you use it so that you don't embarrass anyone or put people on the spot.

Question 2: Verse 1 introduces the historical setting of this book. Summarize the background information for the book of Isaiah from the introduction to this guide. You may want to add more information from a commentary or study Bible.

Question 3: For the significance of the comparison of God's people with Sodom and Gomorrah, ask two volunteers to read Genesis 18:20 and 19:24–25.

Question 6: Isaiah wasn't the only prophet to condemn God's people like this. See also Amos 5:21–24 and Matthew 23.

Question 17: Oak trees and gardens were connected with idol worship and adultery committed in the guise of worship.

"Consider the Message": This section is designed for individual reading outside the group setting.

"Apply the Truth": Be sure to allow enough time for these questions. Depending on the type of question, you may want to have group members respond verbally or record their answers individually. Encourage them to memorize the verse(s) each week.

2: GOD'S FAITHFULNESS CALLS US TO SPIRITUAL CLEANSING AND TO SERVICE: ISAIAH 6

Purpose: To confess sin and respond to God's call for service.

Question 2: King Uzziah died in 740 B.C.

Isaiah's vision would have reminded him of the Holy of Holies in the Temple, especially at the time of its dedication under King Solomon (2 Chronicles 5:13–14; 7:1–13), and God's giving of the law to Moses on Mount Sinai (Exodus 19:18–20).

Seraphs are angels. Their name literally means "burning ones."

Question 4: Compare Isaiah's response to encountering God with how we generally react when we meet Him in His Word. You might want to discuss why we don't have the same reaction.

Question 6: The live coal from the altar symbolized the sin offering, which was burned for atonement from sins.

Conclusion: Print verse 8 in large type on half sheets of paper. Give one to each group member to post at home as a prayer reminder.

3: GOD'S FAITHFULNESS ELICITS PRAISE: ISAIAH 26

Purpose: To praise God for who He is and what He can do.

Question 2: A strong city indicates physical salvation and security.

Question 7: *Waiting* in the Old Testament meant to look forward to something with expectation and hope. Waiting on the Lord was never passive but was accompanied by walking with Him, doing His will, obeying His Word.

Question 12: Verse 17 indicates that Judah's suffering was in vain; it "gave birth to wind," not salvation, which could only come through the Messiah's suffering.

4: GOD'S FAITHFULNESS GIVES US CONFIDENCE IN HIM: ISAIAH 30

Purpose: To increase confidence in God rather than self.

Question 2: This chapter and chapter 31 point out the foolishness of King Hezekiah in making an alliance with Egypt against Assyria. Egypt was no longer a world power and wasn't a threat to Assyria. But instead of asking God for help and protection, the people turned to another country.

Question 8: The salvation God offered His people if they would return to Him meant deliverance from their enemies.

Question 12: Topheth was another name for the Valley of Hinnom outside Jerusalem, where people burned their young children as sacrifices to the pagan god Molech.

5: GOD'S FAITHFULNESS IS REVEALED IN HIS GREATNESS: ISAIAH 40

Purpose: To praise God for His greatness.

Question 2: When an important person was coming to town, people would prepare the way by smoothing out bumps in the road ("every mountain and hill made low") and filling in holes ("every valley shall be raised up"). This custom was applied to the people's journey back to Israel from Babylon and also to John the Baptist's preparation for Jesus' ministry (Matthew 3:3).

Question 4: The name *Sovereign Lord* focuses on God's greatness, power, and rule.

Question 5: The picture of God's two arms—one powerful, one comforting—indicates tough love. A shepherd carried his lambs when they were sick or too tired to walk.

Question 17: This chapter on God's greatness demands a time of praise. Plan your session so you will have time to praise God together after the Bible study, perhaps asking one or two people who are good readers to read the entire chapter aloud before doing so. Close by singing together "How Great Thou Art" or "Our God Is an Awesome God."

6: GOD'S FAITHFULNESS TRANSFORMS US INTO VESSELS HE CAN USE: ISAIAH 45

Purpose: To cooperate with God's work in our lives to be more useful for Him.

Question 2: Although "his anointed" literally means Messiah, it also refers to David and Solomon, who were chosen and commissioned to be kings over God's people.

Question 12: This passage gives two of God's purposes for Cyrus. The third is found in 44:28b. Ask a volunteer to read this verse and its fulfillment in Ezra 1:1–4.

Some of your group members may question God's using an unbeliever to accomplish His will. You might want to discuss this situation for a few minutes, but don't let it eat up too much time. The fact that God works this way highlights the importance of praying for people in all levels of government; see 1 Timothy 2:1–3.

Question 13: Cush is modern-day Ethiopia, and Sabea may be Sheba, in northern Saudi Arabia.

7: GOD'S FAITHFULNESS ENABLES US TO OVERCOME OUR DEPENDENCE ON IDOLS: ISAIAH 46

Purpose: To cast off man-made burdens and idols that have taken God's place in our lives.

Question 2: Bel was another name for Marduk, the sun god. His son, Nebo, was the god of learning, writing, and astronomy. People carried large, heavy images of these gods during festivals, and doing so was "burdensome."

Question 8: Spend some time discussing the issue of modern-day idols. Anything and anyone who takes God's place of supreme importance in our lives is an idol, even if it's not carved in wood or stone.

Question 10: "The former things" referred to the time the Israelites spent wandering in the wilderness, traveling to the land God promised them.

Point out that God repeatedly said throughout this book, "I am God, and there is no other; I am God, and there is none like me." You might want to encourage your group members to look for these phrases as they read through Isaiah. As far as God is concerned, there is no "freedom of religion"; He's the only God.

8: GOD'S FAITHFULNESS ENDURES FOREVER: ISAIAH 51

Purpose: To look for God's faithfulness in our lives and praise Him for it.

Question 2: You might want to take time to identify what God had done for His people in the past.

Discuss how remembering what God has done in the past encourages us when going through tough times in the present.

Question 9: In verse 9, Rahab was a mythological monster that represented Egypt, from where God brought the Israelites out of slavery.

Question 10: For background on the Exodus, read Exodus 14.

Conclusion: End by singing together "Great Is Thy Faithfulness."

9: GOD'S FAITHFULNESS GAVE US A SAVIOR: ISAIAH 52:13–53:12

Purpose: To examine how Jesus' death has changed our lives and to praise God for giving Him as our Savior from sin.

Question 3: Briefly discuss how this description compares to pictures of Jesus' crucifixion.

Question 12: You might want to ask volunteers to read the following passages to show the fulfillment of these verses: Matthew 27:11–14, 57–60; 1 Peter 2:21–23.

Question 14: Read Hebrews 2:9–10 and 1 Peter 2:24–25 for the fulfillment of this prophecy.

Conclusion: Sing together, or read the words to, the hymn "Hallelujah! What a Savior!" which summarizes this portion of Isaiah.

10: GOD'S FAITHFULNESS SATISFIES OUR DEEPEST NEEDS: ISAIAH 55

Purpose: To accept God's invitation for salvation and fulfillment.

Question 2: Be certain group members understand that salvation is a free gift from God. We cannot buy it or work for it. See also Ephesians 2:8–10.

Question 6: The everlasting covenant is described in 2 Samuel 7:11b–16. God promised that David's kingly line would last forever, which will be fulfilled in Jesus the Messiah when He will one day rule this earth.

Question 9: God's invitation for salvation—physically and spiritually—will one day run out. When His judgment begins, it will be too late.

Question 13: In the future messianic kingdom, the effects of sin will be reversed. Have someone read Genesis 3:17–19 to show the contrast.

11: GOD'S FAITHFULNESS GUIDES US: ISAIAH 58

Purpose: To live in such a way that God can easily guide us.

Question 5: The Jewish people were familiar with fasting since fasts were prescribed for a variety of reasons, such as expressing grief (1 Samuel 31:13), demonstrating repentance (Jonah 3:5–10), and observing the Day of Atonement (Leviticus 16:29–31). The latter is the only reason commanded in God's law.

It was a sin not to share food with the poor and needy. Often God uses our actions toward the poor as proof of our love for Him.

Question 6: Be sensitive to people who can't fast for health reasons (i.e., diabetics, hypoglycemics). Talk about other things we can fast from besides food, such as TV, newspaper reading, and e-mail.

Question 10: The word *Sabbath* means rest. The Sabbath was a day set aside for physical relief from work and a time of worshiping God. Keeping it was supposed to mean putting God first—before work, pleasure, etc. However, since breaking the Sabbath was punishable by death (Numbers 15:32–36), probably many people in Isaiah's day kept the Sabbath more out of fear than anything else.

12: GOD'S FAITHFULNESS CHOOSES US AND DELIGHTS IN US: ISAIAH 62

Purpose: To know God chose us and delights in us and to let that truth change our behavior.

Question 4: Names of people and places were important in the Middle East. They often communicated character. So when God gave Jerusalem a new name, He was also changing its character from sinful to righteous.

Question 6: Watchmen were stationed on city walls to look for enemies and to sound warnings if they spotted any. While on duty they were to stay awake at all times.

Question 10: These commands convey a sense of urgency. To "raise a banner" was a way to post an announcement.

Question 12: The last two verses of this chapter summarize the fulfillment of God's salvation and the message of the book of Isaiah.

Endnotes

Introduction
1. Charles Swindoll, *God's Masterwork, Vol. II* (Nashville: Word Publishing, 1997), 86.
2. Henrietta Mears, *What the Bible Is All About* (Ventura, Calif.: Regal Books, 1953), 227.

Session Two
1. *The Book of Isaiah Chapters 1–39* (Grand Rapids, Mich.: William B. Eerdmans, 1986), 186.
2. Charles Swindoll, *God's Masterwork, Vol. II*, 96.
3. J. I. Packer, *Rediscovering Holiness* (Ann Arbor, Mich.: Servant Publications, 1999), 123.

Session Four
1. A. W. Tozer, *The Knowledge of the Holy* (San Francisco: HarperSanFrancisco, 1978).

Session Five
1. Andrew Murray, *Waiting on God* (Minneapolis: Bethany House Publishers, 2001), 14.

Session Six
1. Andrew Murray, *Humility* (Minneapolis: Bethany House Publishers, 2001), 15.
2. Jerry Bridges, *Trusting God* (Colorado Springs: Nav Press, 1988), 52.
3. Adapted from *Becoming a Vessel God Can Use* (Minneapolis: Bethany House Publishers, 1996), 81–83.

Session Seven
1. Adapted from *Living in Absolute Freedom* (Minneapolis: Bethany House Publishers, 2000), 67–69.

Session Nine
1. Beth Moore, *Jesus, the One and Only* (Nashville: Broadman & Holman, 2002), 313.
2. Max Lucado, *He Chose the Nails* (Nashville: W. Publishing, 2002), 113.
3. Quoted in Lucado, *He Chose the Nails*, 58.
4. Adapted from *Living in Absolute Freedom*, 26.

Session Ten
1. Adapted from *This Isn't the Life I Signed Up For* (Minneapolis: Bethany House Publishers, 2003), 146–51.

Session Eleven
1. Adapted from *Standing Firm* (Minneapolis: Bethany House Publishers, 2002), 30–31.

Session Twelve
1. From *Living in Absolute Freedom*, 179–80.

Bibliography

Motyer, J. Alec. *Isaiah.* Downer's Grove, Ill.: InterVarsity Press, 1999.

Oswalt, John N. *Isaiah (The NIV Application Commentary).* Grand Rapids, Mich.: Zondervan, 2003.

Wiersbe, Warren W. *Be Comforted.* Colorado Springs: Cook Communications, 1992.

1. God's Faithfulness Delivers Us From Hypocrisy
Isaiah 1:17–18

Learn to do right!
Seek justice,
encourage the oppressed.
Defend the cause of the fatherless,
plead the case of the widow.
"Come now, let us reason together,"
says the Lord.
"Though your sins are like scarlet,
they shall be as white as snow;
though they are red as crimson,
they shall be like wool."

Extracting the Precious From Isaiah, Donna Partow

2. God's Faithfulness Calls Us to Spiritual Cleansing and to Service
Isaiah 6:5–8

"Woe to me!" I cried. "I am ruined! For I am a man of unclean lips, and I live among a people of unclean lips, and my eyes have seen the King, the Lord Almighty." Then one of the seraphs flew to me with a live coal in his hand, which he had taken with tongs from the altar. With it he touched my mouth and said, "See, this has touched your lips; your guilt is taken away and your sin atoned for." Then I heard the voice of the Lord saying, "Whom shall I send? And who will go for us?" And I said, "Here am I. Send me!"

Extracting the Precious From Isaiah, Donna Partow

3. God's Faithfulness Elicits Praise
Isaiah 26:3–4

You will keep in perfect peace
him whose mind is steadfast,
because he trusts in you.
Trust in the Lord forever,
for the Lord, the Lord,
is the Rock eternal.

Extracting the Precious From Isaiah, Donna Partow

4. God's Faithfulness Gives Us Confidence in Him
Isaiah 30:15, 21

This is what the Sovereign Lord, the Holy One of Israel, says: "In repentance and rest is your salvation, in quietness and trust is your strength." . . . .
Whether you turn to the right or to the left, your ears will hear a voice behind you, saying, "This is the way; walk in it."

Extracting the Precious From Isaiah, Donna Partow

5. God's Faithfulness Is Revealed by His Greatness
Isaiah 40:29–31

He gives strength to the weary
and increases the power of the weak.
Even youths grow tired and weary,
and young men stumble and fall;
but those who hope in the Lord
will renew their strength.
They will soar on wings like eagles;
they will run and not grow weary,
they will walk and not be faint.

Extracting the Precious From Isaiah, Donna Partow

6. God's Faithfulness Transforms Us Into Vessels He Can Use
Isaiah 45:9

Woe to him who quarrels with his Maker, to him who is but a potsherd among the potsherds on the ground. Does the clay say to the potter, "What are you making?" Does your work say, "He has no hands"?

Extracting the Precious From Isaiah, Donna Partow

10. God's Faithfulness Satisfies Our Deepest Needs
Isaiah 55:10–11

As the rain and the snow
come down from heaven,
and do not return to it
without watering the earth
and making it bud and flourish,
so that it yields seed for the sower
and bread for the eater,
so is my word that goes out from my mouth:
It will not return to me empty,
but will accomplish what I desire
and achieve the purpose for which I sent it.

Extracting the Precious From Isaiah, Donna Partow

7. God's Faithfulness Enables Us to Overcome Our Dependence Upon Idols
Isaiah 46:4

Even to your old age and gray hairs I am he,
I am he who will sustain you.
I have made you and I will carry you;
I will sustain you and I will rescue you.

Extracting the Precious From Isaiah, Donna Partow

11. God's Faithfulness Guides Us
Isaiah 58:11

The Lord will guide you always;
he will satisfy your needs in a
sun-scorched land
and will strengthen your frame.
You will be like a well-watered garden,
like a spring whose waters never fail.

Extracting the Precious From Isaiah, Donna Partow

8. God's Faithfulness Endures Forever
Isaiah 51:6–7

But my salvation will last forever,
my righteousness will never fail.
Hear me, you who know what is right,
you people who have my law in your hearts:
Do not fear the reproach of men
or be terrified by their insults.

Extracting the Precious From Isaiah, Donna Partow

12. God's Faithfulness Chooses Us and Delights in Us
Isaiah 62:11–12

The Lord has made proclamation
to the ends of the earth:
"Say to the Daughter of Zion,
'See, your Savior comes!
See, his reward is with him,
and his recompense accompanies him.'"
They will be called the Holy People,
the Redeemed of the Lord;
and you will be called Sought After,
the City No Longer Deserted.

Extracting the Precious From Isaiah, Donna Partow

9. God's Faithfulness Gave Us a Savior
Isaiah 53:5–6

But he was pierced for our transgressions,
he was crushed for our iniquities;
the punishment that brought us peace was
upon him,
and by his wounds we are healed.
We all, like sheep, have gone astray,
each of us has turned to his own way,
and the Lord has laid on him
the iniquity of us all.

Extracting the Precious From Isaiah, Donna Partow

2 CORINTHIANS

For Further study...

Donna Partow's Extracting the Precious Bible study guides help you discover for yourself what God's Word teaches. Each title helps you apply God's truth to your daily life.

Mine Deep Wisdom From Paul's Letter to Corinth

In Partow's 2 Corinthians Bible study guide, discover the life-changing power of sincere faith, which results from a right relationship with God.